Home
Malay Cooking

Rohani Jelani

PERIPLUS

Anyone observing Malay cooks preparing a meal for their family will be easily persuaded that Homestyle Malay Cooking is a simple art. Working calmly and effortlessly, home cooks take a pinch of this and a handful of that, and confidently combine ingredients without hesitation or need to refer to notes, recipe clippings or cookbooks. For everything they need to know is stored in their memory, exactly the way their mother or favourite aunt taught it, all those years ago.

Malay cuisine, with its heavy reliance on herbs, chillies and spices, may look dauntingly exotic to the uninitiated, but once you acquaint yourself with the different ingredients and understand how they work together to create the right balance of harmony and flavour, you will find Malay dishes simple to put together.

Provincial or *kampung* cooking reflects the resourcefulness of the Malay people. Many dishes which in modern times are considered unusual are, in fact, just clever ways to use humble and plentiful ingredients. Fern shoots gathered from the riverbanks are turned into piquant salads. The green unripe fruit of the papaya tree which seems to sprout without any apparent effort within every neighbourhood garden, is slipped into soups and curries. And the banana flower that would otherwise be left to decompose into the ground, is skilfully blended into rich curries and perky salads.

In this collection of recipes, we are sure that you will find a great number of traditional Malay dishes which you can easily duplicate in your modern kitchen. To save you time and effort, we have simplified certain steps and allowed for the use of modern kitchen appliances such as electric choppers and blenders. But we have also made sure that none of these "short cuts" have in any way compromised the taste and authenticity of the original recipes from which they were derived. We hope you enjoy these traditional flavours, cooked the easy, new-fashioned way.

Glossary

Wild pepper leaf (*daun kaduk*): A popular ingredient in the cuisine of Malays in north Malaysia, wild pepper leaf is used in several herb rice dishes.

Carambola (*belimbing asam*): A small green acidic fruit which lends a sour note to curries and pickles. Not to be confused with the larger, sweet, five-edged yellow-green starfruit (*belimbing manis*) of the same family.

Chillies: The most common varieties used in Malay cooking are the medium-sized red (ripe) or green (immature) chillies (*cili*), the tiny hot bird's-eye chillies (*cili padi*), and dried red chillies (*cili kering*).

Chinese celery (*daun sup*): Smaller and more pungent than Western celery. Substitute with Western celery leaves if not available.

Coconut milk (*santan*): To obtain fresh thick coconut milk, add 125 ml (1/2 cup) water to the grated flesh of one coconut and squeeze. To obtain fresh thin coconut milk, squeeze the grated flesh with another 625 ml (2 1/2 cups) water. Powdered coconut milk is readily available in large supermarkets and Asian food stores.

Galangal (*lengkuas*): Resembling pink-coloured ginger, galangal imparts a distinctive flavour to many dishes.

Kaffir lime leaf (*daun limau purut*): Shaped like a figure of eight, this lime leaf adds an intense fragrance to dishes. Sometimes sold as 'fragrant lime leaf'.

Lemongrass (*serai*): Only use the bottom 8 cm or 3 inches of the bulb. Dried lemongrass is available but it is better to look for the fresh variety.

Pandanus (*daun pandan*): Also known as screwpine leaf, pandanus leaves are used to add fragrance to savoury dishes, and green colour to sweet dishes.

Polygonum (*daun laksa, daun kesum*): Also known as laksa leaf or Vietnamese mint, this strongly flavoured herb has long, arrow-shaped leaves.

Shrimp paste (*belacan*): Dried shrimp paste comes in a block which must be cooked before eating. Either bake in the oven, dry fry or hold over a naked flame on the back of a spoon. The end result is the same: it should be dry and crumbly, with a strong aroma. Use sparingly if not accustomed to the aroma.

Tamarind (*asam*): Widely available in pulp form. To obtain 60 ml (1/4 cup) tamarind juice, soak 2 tablespoons pulp with water for 5 minutes. Squeeze the pulp with your fingers, then stir and strain to remove solids. Retain the tamarind juice. Some recipes call for *asam gelugor* or *asam keping* which are dried slices of a sour fruit (L. *garcinia atnoviridis*) but if these are not available, use tamarind pulp.

Torch ginger bud (*bunga kantan, bunga siantan*): The pale pink bud of this wild ginger is particularly aromatic and is popular in many salads. Since there is no real substitute, simply omit it from the recipe if not available.

Yam bean (*bengkuang*): A light brown coloured tuber with a crisp white interior. Also known as jicama.

Sup Tulang
(Beef Rib Soup)

1 kg (2 lb) beef ribs or oxtail, cut into large chunks, fat removed

4 cm (1 1/2 in) fresh ginger, scraped and bruised

4 large cloves garlic, peeled and bruised

3 litres (12 cups) water

2 onions, cut into wedges

2 tomatoes, cut into wedges

2 potatoes, peeled and cut into chunks

1 carrot, scraped and thickly sliced

1–1 1/2 teaspoons salt

4 tablespoons deep-fried shallots

4 tablespoons thinly sliced spring onion

2 tablespoons thinly sliced Chinese celery (*daun sup*)

Spice bag

1 tablespoon coriander seeds

2 teaspoons cumin

2 teaspoons fennel seeds

1 teaspoon black peppercorns

4 cm (1 1/2 in) cinnamon stick

4 whole cardamom pods

8 cloves

2 whole star anise

1. Dry roast all the spice bag ingredients in a small frying pan over low heat until crisp and fragrant, but not browned, about 6 minutes. Use a mortar and pestle or spice grinder to process to a powder. Wrap spices in a small square of muslin, securing tightly with string.
2. Place spice bag, beef, ginger and garlic in a large pan and add water. Bring to the boil, skimming off any fat and scum that rises to the surface. Reduce heat, cover and simmer gently until tender, about 2 hours.
3. When beef is tender, remove spice bag, garlic and ginger. Add onion, tomato, potato, carrot and 1 teaspoon salt. Bring to the boil, cover and simmer until vegetables are tender. Taste and add more salt if necessary.
4. Serve soup piping hot, garnished with fried shallots spring onion and Chinese celery.

If using a pressure cooker, reduce the liquid from 3 litres to 1.5 litres and cook under full pressure for 30 minutes. Proceed to step 3 and continue cooking without pressure.

Serves 4
Preparation time: 20 mins
Cooking time: 3 hours

Masak Singgang Ikan
(Sour Fish Soup)

4 whole small mackerel
(*ikan kembong*), about
600 g (1 lb 3 oz), or
4 Spanish mackerel
steaks (*ikan tenggiri*)
750 ml (3 cups) water,
or more if required
1 teaspoon salt
4 dried tamarind slices
(*asam keping*), or
4 tablespoons tamarind
juice (see page 3)
6 shallots, sliced
4 cloves garlic, sliced
1 cm (1/2 in) galangal,
sliced
2 fresh red chillies, halved
lengthwise, or 8 whole
bird's-eye chillies

1. If using whole fish, clean thoroughly and remove any blood clots.
2. Place water, salt, dried tamarind slices, shallots, garlic, galangal and chillies in a wide saucepan and bring to the boil. Lower heat and simmer for 10 minutes.
3. Add fish and simmer gently until just cooked, 8 to 10 minutes, depending on size and thickness of the fish.
4. Serve soup with rice.

Serves 4
Preparation time: 10 mins
Cooking time: 25 mins

Masak Titik Betik
(Spicy Green Papaya Soup with Prawns)

1/2 medium unripe
   papaya, about 500 g
   (1/2 lb)
1 teaspoon dried shrimp
   paste (*belacan*)
2–3 fresh red chillies,
   chopped
4 shallots, chopped
1 litre (4 cups) water
1 teaspoon salt
150 g (5 oz) medium raw
   prawns, peeled and
   deveined

Serves 4
Preparation time: **20 mins**
Cooking time: **30 mins**

1. Peel the papaya, cut lengthwise into 4 cm (1 1/2 in) widths, then cut across in 1 cm (1/2 in) slices.
2. Wrap the shrimp paste in foil and toast on both sides in a dry wok, until it is dry and crumbly, about 5 minutes.
3. Process shrimp paste, chillies and shallots to a coarse paste using a blender, or mortar and pestle.
4. Put processed mixture in a large pan. Add the water, bring to the boil, cover and simmer 10 minutes.
5. Add the papaya slices, return to the boil, cover and simmer until just tender, about 10 minutes. Season to taste with salt.
6. Add prawns and simmer until just cooked, about 3 minutes. Serve hot with rice.

Bubur Lambuk
(Savoury Rice Porridge)

200 g (1 cup) rice
2 1/2 litres (10
  cups) water
4 cm (1 1/2 in)
  cinnamon
1 whole star anise
4 cloves
3 cm (1 1/4 in)
  fresh ginger,
  scraped and
  bruised
150 g (5 oz) lean
  beef, minced or
  coarsely chopped
10 black pepper-
  corns
100 g (3 1/2 oz)
  boneless chicken,
  cut into small dice
150 g (5 oz)
  medium-sized raw
  prawns, peeled,
  deveined and cut
  into small dice
185 ml (3/4 cup)
  coconut milk
  (optional)
Salt to taste
4 tablespoons
  deep-fried shallots
2 tablespoons
  chopped spring
  onion

1. Wash rice in several changes of water. Drain and put in a large pan. Add water and bring to the boil.
2. Add whole spices, ginger and beef. Partially cover with lid and simmer gently, stirring several times, about 1 hour or until rice is very soft and creamy. If rice porridge starts to dry out, add a little hot water.
3. When rice is soft, remove cinnamon, star anise and ginger. Add chicken and prawns and simmer for 15 minutes.
4. Add the coconut milk, if used, and season to taste with salt. Serve hot, garnished with fried shallots and spring onion.

The rice should be cooked until the grains are broken and the texture is smooth, soft and creamy.

Serves 4
Preparation time: **15 mins**
Cooking time: **1 hour 15 mins**

Nasi Kerabu
(Herb Rice)

100 g (1 cup loosely-packed) grated fresh or desiccated coconut

50 g (1 3/4 oz) salt fish

2 tablespoons oil

375 g (3 cups) cold cooked rice, separated with a fork

40 g (1 cup) finely shredded mixed herbs (see note)

1 stem lemongrass, inner part of bottom 10 cm (4 in) only, very thinly sliced

1 torch ginger bud (*bunga kantan*), thinly sliced (optional)

10 shallots, thinly sliced

2 cm (3/4 in) fresh young ginger, finely shredded

1 cm (1/2 in) young galangal, finely shredded

1 cm (1/2 in) fresh turmeric, finely shredded, or 1/2 teaspoon turmeric powder

1/2 teaspoon salt, or more to taste

1/2 teaspoon freshly ground black pepper

1. Dry-fry the grated coconut in a wok over very low heat until golden brown, stirring constantly to prevent burning, about 20 minutes for fresh coconut, 10 minutes for desiccated. Cool slightly. Pound with a mortar and pestle, or process in a food processor until it is the texture of fine breadcrumbs.

2. Rinse the salt fish under running water to remove excess salt. Dry with paper towel. Heat the oil in a small frying pan and fry salt fish over low heat until lightly coloured on both sides, about 2 minutes. Cool and shred finely.

3. Combine the rice with all the rest of the ingredients in a large bowl, mixing with two wooden spoons or clean hands. Adjust salt to taste. Serve as soon as possible after mixing. Can be served with Ayam Percik (page 44), Sambal Tumis Udang (page 41) or Rendang Daging (page 54).

Bunches of mixed herbs (daun ulam) especially for this dish are sold in Malay market stalls and include long-stemmed mint (daun kesum or daun laksa), Asian pennywort (daun pegaga), aromatic ginger leaf (daun cekur), common mint (daun pudina), kaffir lime leaf (daun limau purut), young cashew leaves (daun cajus), wild pepper leaf (daun kaduk) and ulam raja. Substitutes could include dill, celery leaf, young passion fruit leaf, watercress, nasturtium leaf and coriander leaf. To shred the herbs, wash and pat dry with a clean cloth. Roll up a wad of herbs using the larger leaves on the outside. Shred very finely, using a very sharp knife.

Serves 4
Preparation time: **25 mins**
Cooking time: **30 mins**

Nasi Kunyit
(Yellow Rice)

400 g (2 cups) glutinous white rice

2 pieces fresh turmeric root, each 7 cm (3 in) long (about 40 g), or 1 tablespoon ground turmeric

3 dried tamarind slices (*asam keping/asam gelugor*)

6–8 pandanus leaves, or few drops of pandan essence

1 cup (250 ml) thick coconut milk

1 1/2 teaspoons salt

1/2 teaspoon black or white peppercorns (optional)

Serves 4
Preparation time: **15 mins + 4 hours soaking**
Cooking time: **1 hour**

1. Pick rice over and discard grit or foreign particles. Put rice in a bowl, cover with water and rub with the fingers. Drain and repeat several times until water runs clear. Place rice in a large bowl with water to cover by about 8 cm.

2. Scrape the skin off the turmeric, chop coarsely, then grind to a paste in a spice grinder or with a mortar and pestle until fine. Tie the pounded turmeric in a small square of muslin. Bury turmeric bag and tamarind slices in the rice and soak at room temperature 4 hours, or overnight if preferred.

3. Rinse rice and drain in a colander, discarding the bag of turmeric and tamarind slices.

4. Line a steaming basket with an old tea towel (it may be stained yellow), pandanus leaf or muslin. Place pandanus slices on top, cutting to fit in the steamer and cover the tea towel completely. Spoon over the drained rice evenly. Put steamer on top of rapidly boiling water and steam 30 minutes.

5. Combine salt and coconut milk in a large bowl. Add rice, discarding the pandanus leaves, and stir well with a wooden spoon until all the coconut milk has been absorbed. Stir in the peppercorns, if used.

6. Spread rice over the tea towel in the steamer and cook 30 minutes. Take steamer off the heat and transfer rice onto serving dish.

Nasi Dagang
(East Coast Traders' Rice)

400 g (2 cups) red glutinous rice (see note)
6–8 pandanus leaves, or few drops of pandan essence
1 1/2 teaspoons salt
1 cup (250 ml) thick coconut milk
1/4 teaspoon fenugreek seeds
1 1/2 cm (1 3/4 in) fresh ginger, finely shredded
3 shallots, thinly sliced

Serves 4
Preparation time: **15 mins** + **4 hours soaking**
Cooking time: **50 mins**

1. Soak rice for several hours, preferably overnight. Drain, cover with water again and rub with the fingers. Drain and repeat several times. Place rice in a large bowl with water to cover by about 8 cm.
2. Line a steaming basket with a tea towel or muslin. Place pandanus leaves on top, cutting to fit in the steamer, covering the tea towel completely. Spoon the drained rice evenly over the leaves. Put steamer on top of rapidly boiling water and steam 30 minutes.
3. Combine salt and coconut milk in a large bowl. Add rice, discard the pandanus leaves, and stir well with a wooden spoon until all the coconut milk has been absorbed. Stir in the fenugreek seeds, ginger and shallots.
4. Spread rice over the tea towel in the steamer and cook 30 minutes. Take steamer off the heat and transfer rice onto serving dish.

A special red glutinous rice, available on the east coast of Peninsular Malaysia, is normally used for this dish. If this is not available, use 200 g (1 cup) long-grain rice and 200 g (1 cup) glutinous white rice and omit the soaking step (rinse and steam directly). If using pandan essence, add in step 3 together with the coconut milk.

Nasi Goreng
(Spicy Fried Rice with Long Beans)

2 fresh red chillies,
  chopped
4–5 cloves garlic,
  chopped
3 shallots, chopped
1/2 teaspoon dried
  shrimp paste
  (*belacan*)
2 tablespoons oil
200 g (7 oz) medium-
  sized raw prawns,
  peeled, deveined
  and diced, or 100 g
  (3 1/2 oz) chicken
  breast, diced
1/2 teaspoon salt
Freshly ground black
  pepper

1/2 teaspoon sugar
60 g (1/2 cup) diced
  long beans
250 g (2 cups) cold
  cooked rice, broken up
  with a fork

Serves 4
Preparation time: **15 mins**
Cooking time: **15 mins**

1. Process chillies, garlic, shallots and dried shrimp
   paste to a smooth paste in a spice grinder, adding a
   little of the oil if necessary to keep mixture turning.
2. Heat oil in a wok and fry the ground ingredients
   over low to moderate heat, stirring frequently, until
   fragrant and the oil surfaces, about 5 minutes.
3. Increase heat slightly. Add the prawns or chicken,
   sprinkle with salt, pepper and sugar, and stir-fry
   over moderate heat for 2 minutes. Add the long
   beans and stir-fry for 2 minutes.
4. Add rice and stir-fry for 5 to 6 minutes.

Sambal Telur
(Eggs in Chilli Sauce)

4 hard-boiled eggs,
  peeled
8–10 dried chillies
4 fresh red chillies,
  seeds and membranes
  discarded
6 shallots, chopped
4 tablespoons oil
2 teaspoons lime juice
1–1 1/2 teaspoons
  sugar
1 teaspoon salt

Serves 4
Preparation time: **15 mins**
Cooking time: **20 mins**

1. Cut dried chillies into 2-cm (3/4-in) lengths, soak in warm water until softened, 10 to 15 minutes. Rub with fingers to dislodge as many seeds as possible, then lift out chillies and discard water and seeds.
2. Process soaked chillies, fresh chillies and shallots to a smooth paste in a blender, adding a little oil if needed to keep the mixture turning.
3. Heat the oil in a wok and add ground ingredients. Cook over low heat, stir frequently until chilli paste is cooked and oil separates, about 10 minutes.
4. Stir in lime juice, salt and sugar to taste.
5. Cut eggs in half lengthwise. Place on a serving dish and spoon over the cooked chilli paste.

Some cooks deep-fry the shelled whole eggs as this gives them a crisp coating.

Masak Lemak Nangka
(Young Jackfruit in Coconut Milk)

350 g (11 1/2 oz)
  peeled young jackfruit,
  cut into bite-sized
  pieces
4–8 bird's-eye chillies
3–4 shallots
1 1/2 cm (1 1/4 in)
  fresh turmeric root, or
  1 teaspoon ground
  turmeric
200 g (6 1/4 oz) bone-
  less chicken, cut into
  bite-sized pieces
375 ml (1 1/2 cups)
  coconut milk
1 teaspoon salt
1 dried tamarind slice
  (*asam keping*)
1 small turmeric leaf

Serves 4
Preparation time: **15 mins**
Cooking time: **45 mins**

1. Bring a large saucepan of water to the boil. Add
   jackfruit pieces and boil until just tender, 8 to 10
   minutes. Drain and set aside.
2. While jackfruit is cooking, process the chillies,
   shallots and turmeric to a smooth paste in a
   blender. Transfer to a large saucepan and add
   the chicken. Cook over medium heat, stirring
   frequently, for 15 minutes.
3. Add the coconut milk, salt and jackfruit. Bring to
   the boil, stirring constantly, then simmer uncovered
   over low heat for 15 minutes, stirring from time to
   time.
4. Add the salt, tamarind and turmeric leaf. Simmer
   5 minutes and then take the pan off the heat.

Kerabu Pucuk Paku
(Fern Tip Salad)

500–600 g (1 lb) fern shoots (substitute with English spinach)

2 tablespoons dried prawns, soaked in hot water 5 minutes, drained

100 g (1 cup lightly packed) grated fresh coconut, or 60 g (3/4 cup) desiccated coconut

1 tablespoon dried tamarind pulp

4 tablespoons warm water

3 red chillies, seeds removed to reduce heat as desired

1/2 teaspoon dried shrimp paste (*belacan*)

1/2 teaspoon salt

1 1/2 teaspoons sugar

1 tablespoon lime juice

1 small red onion or 4–5 shallots, peeled and sliced

1 torch ginger bud (*bunga kantan*), thinly sliced

Serves 4
Preparation time: **25 mins**
Cooking time: **20 mins**

1. Pinch off 5 cm (2 in) of each fern shoot tip. Remove leaves from tough stems, discarding stems to provide about 250 to 300 g (3 cups) tips and leaves. Bring a large saucepan of water to the boil and blanch ferns for 2 minutes. Drain, then refresh under cold running water. Squeeze gently to remove excess moisture, then set aside in colander.

2. Process or pound soaked prawns to a powder using a spice grinder or mortar and pestle. Stir-fry in a dry wok over low heat until crisp, 4 to 5 minutes.

3. Stir-fry coconut in a dry wok over low heat until crisp and golden brown, 20 minutes for fresh coconut, or about 10 minutes for desiccated. Cool slightly before processing to the texture of fine breadcrumbs in a mortar and pestle, or food processor.

4. Soak tamarind in warm water, 5 minutes. Squeeze and strain to obtain juice. Spread shrimp paste in a thin layer on a piece of foil. Toast on both sides in a wok until dry and crumbly, 4 to 5 minutes. Process shrimp paste to a powder in a spice grinder or mortar and pestle. Add chillies, salt and sugar and process until smooth.

5. Put fern shoots, dried prawns, coconut, sliced onion and ginger bud in a large bowl and toss with clean hands to mix thoroughly. Add chilli mixture, tamarind juice and lime juice, and mix well with a spoon and fork. Taste and adjust salt and sugar as desired. Serve as soon as possible.

Discard large stems to leave tips and leaves.

Kerabu Jantung Pisang
(Banana Flower Salad)

- 1 banana flower
- 1 medium-sized mackerel, about 300 g (10 oz)
- 100 g (1 cup) freshly grated or desiccated coconut
- 125 ml (1/2 cup) thick coconut milk
- 1 medium purple onion, halved lengthways and thinly sliced across
- 1 tablespoon lime juice
- 2 teaspoons sugar
- 1 teaspoons salt
- 1/2–1 teaspoon freshly ground black pepper

Serves 4
Preparation time: **20 mins**
Cooking time: **30 mins**

1. Peel off three to four outer layers of the flower until you reach the pale, tender inner bud. Put flower in a large saucepan, cover with water and bring to the boil. Simmer 20 to 25 minutes or until the tip of a knife pierces the centre easily.
2. While banana flower is cooking, put fish in a pan and cover with water. Simmer gently until cooked, about 8 minutes, then drain and cool. Discard skin and bones, and flake flesh coarsely; there should be about 150 g (1 cup) flesh. Set aside.
3. Dry-fry coconut in a wok over low heat, stirring constantly until golden brown, 20 minutes. Cool toasted coconut slightly before pounding in a mortar and pestle or blender until the texture of fine breadcrumbs. Set aside.
4. When banana flower is cooked, quarter lengthwise and leave until cool enough to handle. Squeeze gently to remove excess moisture. Cut at a slight diagonal into 1-cm (1/2-in) slices.
5. Put banana flower, fish and coconut in a mixing bowl. Add coconut milk, onion, lime juice, sugar, salt and pepper and gently mix together. Serve immediately.

Peel the outer layers of the flower until you reach the pale, tender inner bud.

Dry-fry the coconut in a wok over low heat, stirring constantly until golden brown.

Tahu Sumbat
(Stuffed Tofu)

4 pieces firm white tofu,
  600 g (1 1/4 lb)
Salt
250 ml (1 cup) oil
70 g (1/2 cup) finely
  shredded yam bean or
  jicama (*bengkuang*)
70 g (1/2 cup) finely
  shredded cucumber
80 g (1 cup)
  beansprouts

Chilli Sauce
4 fresh red chillies,
  seeded and chopped
2 cloves garlic, chopped
1/2 teaspoon salt
1 1/2 tablespoons sugar
3 tablespoons water
2 tablespoons white
  vinegar
2 tablespoons tomato
  sauce

Serves 4
Preparation time: **20 mins**
Cooking time: **15 mins**

1. Halve each piece of tofu diagonally. Blot carefully with kitchen paper to absorb moisture. Rub a little salt over the tofu.
2. Prepare chilli sauce. Process chillies, garlic, salt and sugar in a blender until coarsely ground. Add water, vinegar and tomato sauce and process until smooth. Put in a sauce bowl.
3. Heat oil in a wok and fry half the tofu, turning until crisp and golden brown on all sides, about 4 minutes. Remove, drain on absorbent paper. Repeat with remaining tofu. When cool, make a horizontal slit on the cut side of each piece of tofu to create a pocket, being careful not to cut through.
4. Blanch beansprouts in boiling water, 10 seconds. Drain and refresh under cold running water. Mix beansprouts, yam bean and cucumber.
5. Stuff each tofu pocket with the shredded vegetables and beansprouts and serve with chilli sauce.

An alternative presentation is to dice the deep-fried tofu, put on a plate and scatter with the shredded vegetables and beansprouts.

Make a horizontal slit on the cut side of each piece of deep-fried tofu.

Stuff each tofu pocket with the shredded vegetables.

Goreng Terung Berlada
(Fried Eggplant with Chilli)

4 medium-sized slender
Asian eggplants
(*terung*), about 500 g
(1 lb)
4 tablespoons oil

Chilli Paste
8–10 dried chillies
1 tablespoon dried
tamarind pulp
4 tablespoons water
2–4 fresh red chillies,
seeds removed as
desired, chopped
6 shallots, chopped
2 cloves garlic, chopped
3 tablespoons oil
2 teaspoons sugar
1 teaspoon salt

Serves 4
Preparation time: 15 mins
Cooking time: 35 mins

1. To make the chilli paste, cut dried chillies into 2-cm (3/4-in) lengths and soak in warm water for 10 to 15 minutes until softened. Rub with the fingers to remove as many seeds as you can, and lift out carefully, leaving seeds in the bowl. Soak tamarind in water, 5 minutes, then squeeze and strain to obtain the juice.
2. Grind the soaked chillies, fresh chillies, shallots and garlic in a spice grinder or blender to obtain a fine paste, adding a little oil if needed to keep the mixture turning.
3. Heat oil in a wok or small frying pan and cook the chilli paste over low heat, stirring frequently, until thoroughly cooked and oil surfaces, about 10 minutes. Add the tamarind juice, sugar and salt and cook 1 minute. Set aside.
4. Remove eggplant stalks and cut each eggplant in half lengthwise. Heat half the oil in a frying pan and fry half the eggplant until cooked and lightly browned, on both sides, about 10 minutes. Drain on absorbent paper. Heat remaining oil and cook the rest of the eggplant.
5. Put eggplant on a serving dish and spoon some chilli sauce over the top of each piece.

If Asian eggplant is not available, use a regular eggplant weighing about 500 g (1 lb) and cut it across in 1-cm (1/2-in) slices, then cook as directed.

Tempe, Tahu & Sayur Goreng
(Tempe & Tofu Stir-fry)

50 g (1 1/2 oz) glass (bean-thread or transparent) noodles, soaked 3–4 minutes in warm water to soften
1 tablespoon dried tamarind pulp
60 ml (1/4 cup) warm water
125 ml (1/2 cup) oil
200 g (2 cups diced) tempe, cut in 1-cm (1/2-in) dice
200 g (2 cups diced) firm tofu, cut in 1-cm (1/2-in) dice
3 cloves garlic, sliced
1 tablespoon finely shredded ginger
1/2 teaspoon dried shrimp paste (*belacan*)
1 stem lemongrass, bottom tender 10 cm (2 in) thinly sliced
200 g (6 1/2 oz) medium-sized raw prawns, peeled and deveined
200 g (6 1/2 oz) lean tender beef, cut in 1-cm (1/2-in) dice
200 g (6 1/2 oz) green beans, tops, tails and strings removed, sliced diagonally in 2-cm (3/4-in) lengths
2 red chillies, sliced or finely shredded
1 teaspoon salt

1. Drain soaked noodles and cut with scissors into 4-cm (1 1/2-in) lengths. Soak tamarind in water 5 minutes, squeeze and strain through a sieve to obtain tamarind juice.
2. Heat oil and fry the tempe over moderate to high heat in 2 batches, stirring until golden brown, about 4 minutes. Drain on absorbent paper. Repeat with tofu.
3. Remove all but 2 tablespoons of oil from the wok. When oil is moderately hot, add garlic and ginger and stir-fry 10 seconds. Add shrimp paste and stir-fry, crumbling the shrimp paste, until garlic is light brown, about 1 minute.
4. Add the lemongrass, prawns and beef, and stir-fry for 5 minutes. Add the green beans, chilli, tempe and tofu. Stir-fry 5 minutes.
5. Add drained glass noodles and salt. Stir-fry until beans are just tender, about 2 more minutes. Add tamarind juice, stir to mix well, then serve.

Serves 4
Preparation time: **35 mins**
Cooking time: **30 mins**

Cucur Udang
(Savoury Prawn Fritters)

125 g (1 cup) plain flour
125 g (1 cup)
  self-raising flour
1 1/2 teaspoons salt
Pinch white pepper
1/4 teaspoon ground
  turmeric
375 ml (1 1/2 cups)
  water, more if required
200 g (6 1/2 oz)
  medium-sized raw
  prawns, peeled,
  deveined and cut in
  1-cm (1/2-in) lengths
1 onion, halved length-
  wise and sliced across
50 g (1/2 cup) Chinese
  chives or spring onion,
  cut to 3-cm (1 1/4-in)
  lengths
50 g (1/4 cup) corn ker-
  nels (fresh, tinned or
  frozen) (optional)
Oil for frying

Serves 4
Preparation time: 20 mins
Cooking time: 20 mins

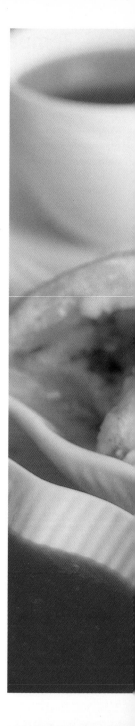

1. Sift the plain and self-raising flour into a mixing
   bowl. Add the salt, pepper and turmeric and stir in
   water to make a thick batter that falls off a spoon
   easily. Mix with a spoon, but do not beat.
2. Stir in prawns, onion, chives and corn kernels (if
   used).
3. Heat 2 cm (3/4 in) oil in a wok or saucepan. Drop
   heaped tablespoons of batter into the hot oil and
   fry until golden brown on both sides, about 4 minutes. Drain on paper towel and serve warm with a
   good chilli sauce.

Solok Cili
(Steamed Green Chillies with Fish Stuffing)

8–10 large green chillies
400 g (13 oz) whole mackerel, or 300 g (10 oz) Spanish mackerel cutlets
1/2 teaspoon black peppercorns
3 shallots, chopped
1 cm (1/2 in) fresh ginger, chopped
1/2 teaspoon salt
1 teaspoon sugar
3 tablespoons freshly grated or desiccated coconut
1 tablespoon lime juice
85 ml (1/3 cup) coconut cream

1. Trim the chilli stalks to about 1 1/2 cm (3/4 in) in length. Split the chillies lengthwise from just beneath the stalk, right down to the tip, being careful not to cut through to the other side. Use a sharp pointed knife to remove the membranes and seeds of each chilli, then rinse to dislodge any remaining seeds. Drain.
2. Clean the fish and poach gently in water to cover until fish is cooked. When cool enough to handle, carefully remove all bones and skin. Flake fish to obtain about 125 g (1 cup loosely packed) flaked fish.
3. Coarsely grind peppercorns in a spice grinder. Add the shallots, ginger, salt and sugar, and process until smooth. Add coconut and lime juice, process for a few seconds to mix well, then put in a bowl. Add fish and stir to mix thoroughly.
4. Stuff the chillies with the fish mixture. Lay stuffed chillies on a heatproof plate, drizzle with the coconut milk and steam for 30 minutes.

Serves 4
Preparation time: **30 mins**
Cooking time: **30 mins**

After trimming the stem, split the chillies lengthwise.

Stuff the chillies with the mixture and place on a heatproof plate.

Masak Lemak Ikan Dengan Belimbing
(Sour Fish Curry)

2 fresh red chillies, chopped

3–6 bird's-eye chillies, chopped

2 cm (3/4 in) fresh turmeric, chopped, or 1 teaspoon ground turmeric

5 shallots, sliced

500 ml (2 cups) coconut milk

500 g (1 lb) fish cutlets or fillets (snapper, Spanish mackerel, or black pomfret), washed and dried

1 teaspoon salt

100 g (about 10) small sour carambola, halved lengthwise

1. Process all the chillies and turmeric to a fine paste in a spice grinder, adding a little of the coconut milk if necessary to keep the mixture turning.
2. Put the chilli paste, shallots and coconut milk in a wide saucepan. Bring to the boil, stirring continuously to prevent coconut milk from curdling
3. Add the fish and salt. Simmer uncovered over low heat for 5 minutes
4. Add the halved carambola and simmer for 10 minutes.

If carambola is not available, use 100 g (about 3) small unripe green mangoes. Halve the mangoes, remove the stone, and quarter. Add to the curry in step 4 but cook for only 5 minutes.

Serves 4
Preparation time: **15 mins**
Cooking time: **10 mins**

Masak Lemak Ketam Dengan Nenas
(Crab & Pineapple in Spicy Coconut Gravy)

1 kg (2 lb) blue swimmer crabs

2 fresh red chillies, sliced

4–8 bird's-eye chillies, sliced

5 shallots, chopped

2 cm (3/4 in) fresh turmeric, chopped, or 1 teaspoon ground turmeric

500 ml (2 cups) coconut milk

1 teaspoon salt

250 g (1 1/2 cups) bite-sized pieces pineapple

1. Lift up the flap on the underside of each crab and pull to remove the back. Remove the finger-like gills and rinse crabs well, removing any muddy bits. Halve the crabs and use a cleaver to crack the claws. Leave to drain in a colander.

2. Process chillies, shallot and turmeric root to a smooth paste in a spice grinder, adding a little coconut milk if needed to keep mixture turning.

3. Put the chilli paste, coconut milk and salt in a wok and bring to the boil over medium heat, stirring all the time to prevent the coconut from curdling. Add the crabs and pineapple and cook for 15 to 20 minutes until crabs turn pink.

Serves 4
Preparation time: **30 mins**
Cooking time: **40 mins**

To obtain 250 g (1 1/2 cups) diced pineapple, peel core and dice half of a small (1 kg) pineapple.

Percik Ikan
(Grilled Fish in Spicy Coconut Paste)

1 large black pomfret,
sea bass or trevally
(about 1–1.25 kg),
or 8 small mackerel
(*ikan kembong*)
1 teaspoon salt
1 teaspoon ground
turmeric

Gravy
8–10 dried chillies, cut
in 2 cm (3/4 in)
lengths
1 tablespoon dried
tamarind pulp
60 ml (1/4 cup) water
6 shallots, roughly
chopped
1/2 teaspoon dried
shrimp paste
(*belacan*)
250 ml (1 cup) thick
coconut milk
1/2 teaspoon salt
1/2 teaspoon sugar

1. Clean fish and dry with kitchen paper. Rub with salt and turmeric and set aside.
2. To prepare the gravy, soak dried chillies in warm water for 10 to 15 minutes until soft. Soak tamarind pulp in warm water, 5 minutes, then squeeze and strain to obtain juice.
3. Drain chillies, then process with shallots and shrimp paste in an electric blender, adding a little of the coconut milk to make a smooth paste. Add the rest of the coconut milk and blend 30 seconds. Pour through a fine strainer into a small wok or pan, pressing the solids against the strainer. Discard the solids.
4. Add tamarind juice to spiced coconut milk, bring to the boil, then simmer uncovered over medium heat, stirring frequently, until gravy thickens and oil starts to separate, about 15 minutes. Season with salt and sugar.
5. Heat a charcoal barbecue or grill. Cook fish over moderate heat, 5 minutes on each side. Spoon gravy over one side of the fish and put this side facing the heat. Cook over low heat, 8 to 10 minutes. Turn, cover other side of fish with gravy and continue cooking until fish is done. Test with the tip of a knife to ensure flesh is white and flakes easily.

Take care heat is not too high when grilling the fish in the final stages or the gravy may burn.

Serves 4
Preparation time: **30 mins**
Cooking time: **45 mins**

Kari Ikan
(Fish Curry)

4–5 cloves garlic, chopped

1 medium-sized onion or 4 shallots, chopped

3 tablespoons fish curry powder

3 tablespoons dried tamarind pulp

560 ml (2 1/4 cups) water

4 tablespoons oil

1 teaspoon black mustard seeds

1/4 teaspoon fenugreek seeds

1/2 teaspoon cumin seeds

1 stalk curry leaves

2 medium tomatoes, each cut into 6 wedges

1 whole black pomfret, grouper or trevally (about 500 g), cut in 4 pieces

8–10 small ladies' fingers (okra), stalk ends removed

4 green chillies, halved lengthwise

125 ml (1/2 cup) coconut milk

1 teaspoon salt

1. Process garlic and onion to a smooth paste in a spice grinder or blender, adding a little oil if needed to keep the mixture turning. Set aside. Mix curry powder with 4 tablespoons of the water to form a paste and set aside.

2. Soak tamarind in remaining 500 ml (2 cups) water for 5 minutes, then squeeze and strain to obtain tamarind juice. Set aside.

3. Heat oil in a wide saucepan. Add mustard seeds, fenugreek, cumin and curry leaves, and fry until the mustard seeds start to pop, about 30 seconds. Add the garlic and onion paste and stir-fry over low heat until the mixture smells fragrant and starts to brown, about 5 minutes.

4. Add curry paste and cook over low heat until dry and the oil starts to separate, 8 to 10 minutes. Add tamarind juice and bring to the boil.

5. Add tomatoes and simmer uncovered for 5 minutes.

6. Add fish and simmer gently, uncovered, for 5 minutes. Add the ladies' fingers, green chillies, coconut milk and salt, and simmer until fish and ladies' fingers are cooked, about 10 minutes.

Instead of using whole fish, you could use 500 g (1 lb) fish fillets or cutlets. Turn fish once or twice during cooking to ensure it cooks evenly.

Serves 4
Preparation time: **15 mins**
Cooking time: **35 mins**

Sambal Tumis Udang
(Chilli-fried Prawns)

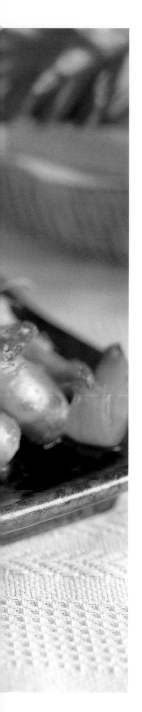

15–20 dried chillies, cut
  in 2-cm (3/4-in) pieces
1 tablespoon dried
  tamarind pulp
125 ml (1/2 cup) water
1/2 teaspoon dried
  shrimp paste (*belacan*)
10 shallots, chopped
4 tablespoons oil
500–600 g (1–1 1/4 lb)
  medium-sized raw
  prawns, peeled,
  deveined and tails left
  intact
3 kaffir lime leaves, edges
  slightly torn (optional)
1 medium onion, cut in
  10 wedges
2 teaspoons sugar
1 teaspoon salt

Serves 4
Preparation time: **30 mins**
Cooking time: **30 mins**

1. Soak the chillies in hot water until soft, 10 to 15 minutes. Rub with the hands to dislodge as many seeds as possible, then lift out chillies, leaving seeds in the bottom of the bowl.
2. Soak tamarind in water for 5 minutes, then squeeze and strain to obtain tamarind juice.
3. Process chillies, shrimp paste and shallots in a spice grinder until fine, adding a little oil if necessary to keep mixture turning.
4. Heat the oil in a wok and add the ground ingredients. Stir-fry over low heat, 6 to 8 minutes, until the oil surfaces.
5. Add tamarind juice and cook over low heat, stirring frequently, for 10 minutes. Add the prawns, kaffir lime leaves and onion wedges, and stir-fry over low to medium heat, 10 minutes. Add sugar and salt and stir until dissolved.

Ayam Goreng Garam Kunyit
(Salt & Turmeric Chicken)

3/4–1 kg (1 1/2–2 lb)
chicken pieces
3 cm (1 1/4 in) fresh
turmeric or 1 1/2 tea-
spoons ground turmeric
1 1/2–2 teaspoons salt
1/2 teaspoon ground
black pepper
125 ml (1/2 cup) oil
1 teaspoon sugar
1 large onion, cut in
1/2 cm (1/4 in) slices,
separated into rings

1. Dry chicken with paper towel and cut into serving pieces.
2. If using turmeric root, process to a paste using a spice grinder or mortar and pestle. Combine turmeric, salt and pepper in a small bowl. Sprinkle over the chicken pieces, mixing to distribute evenly. Marinate 20 minutes.
3. Heat oil in a wok. Add the chicken pieces and cook over high heat to seal in the juices and to brown slightly, 4 minutes. Reduce heat to medium and fry chicken, stirring frequently, 10 minutes.
4. Add sugar and onion rings and cook, stirring frequently, until onion is lightly browned and chicken cooked, 8 to 10 minutes. Remove with a slotted spatula and drain well on paper towel. Serve hot.

Use a mixture of chicken pieces still on the bone, such as drumstick, thigh and breast, or half a medium to large chicken.

Serves 4
Preparation time: **30 mins**
Cooking time: **25 mins**

Ayam Percik
(Kelantan-style BBQ Chicken)

4 medium-sized chicken legs (thighs and drumsticks)
2 cm (3/4 in) fresh ginger, finely ground or grated
1 teaspoon ground turmeric
1 teaspoon salt

Gravy
1 tablespoon dried tamarind pulp
4 tablespoons warm water
8–10 dried chillies, cut in 2 cm (3/4 in) lengths, soaked in hot water until soft
10 shallots, chopped
2 cloves garlic, chopped
1/2 teaspoon dried shrimp paste (*belacan*)
500 ml (2 cups) thick coconut milk
10 fenugreek seeds
1 teaspoon salt
1 teaspoon sugar
1 teaspoon rice flour or cornflour

1. Remove skin and excess fat from chicken, then pat dry with paper towel. Combine the ginger, turmeric and salt and rub all over the chicken. Cover and set aside while preparing gravy.
2. To prepare the gravy, soak tamarind pulp in warm water, 5 minutes, then squeeze and strain to obtain juice. Grind the chillies, shallots, garlic and shrimp paste in an electric blender, adding a little of the coconut milk to make a smooth paste. Add the rest of the coconut milk and blend 30 seconds. Pour through a fine strainer into a wok or pan, pressing the solids against the strainer. Discard the solids.
3. Add tamarind juice, fenugreek, salt, sugar and rice flour to the gravy and cook, stirring frequently, until the sauce is thick and the oil starts to separate, about 15 minutes.
4. Add the chicken thighs and cook uncovered over medium heat, stirring frequently for 20 minutes.
5. Remove chicken and grill over charcoal for about 8 to 10 minutes per side, or until well browned, basting it several times with the remaining gravy. Alternatively, place chicken on a rack in a roasting tin and roast in a preheated 200°C (400°F, Gas 6) oven for about 30 minutes or until chicken is well browned. Baste occasionally with the gravy.
6. Simmer any remaining gravy over low heat until thick and spoon over the cooked chicken. Allow chicken to cool for 10 minutes before cutting into serving pieces.

Serves 4
Preparation time: **35 mins**
Cooking time: **45 mins**

Ayam Goreng Berjintan
(Stir-fried Cumin Chicken)

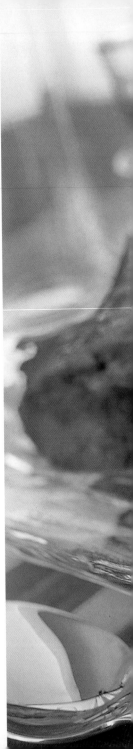

3/4–1 kg (1 1/2–2 lb)
  chicken pieces
1 teaspoon salt
Sprinkling white pepper
1 tablespoon cumin seeds
1 1/2 teaspoons fennel
  seeds
1 teaspoon black pepper-
  corns
2 cm (3/4 in) fresh ginger
5 cloves garlic
3 tablespoons oil
250 ml (1 cup) water

Serves 4
Preparation time: 20 mins
Cooking time: 35 mins

1. Cut chicken into serving pieces. Sprinkle salt and
   pepper on the chicken and set aside.
2. Dry-roast the cumin, fennel and black peppercorns
   over low heat until fragrant and crisp, about
   2 minutes, taking care not to burn. Grind to a
   powder in an electric grinder or mortar and pestle.
   Set aside. Grind the ginger and garlic to a smooth
   paste. Set aside.
3. Heat the oil in a wok and stir-fry the ginger and
   garlic over medium heat, 30 seconds. Add the
   chicken pieces and stir-fry for 10 minutes over
   medium heat.
4. Add the ground spices and stir-fry for 10 minutes
   over medium heat.
5. Add water and bring to the boil. Turn down heat
   and simmer uncovered, stirring frequently, until
   chicken pieces are tender and most of the liquid
   has evaporated, 12 to 15 minutes.

*Remove the chicken skin and all traces of fat to
reduce the cholesterol content of this dish. After
adding the water in step 5, scrape the bottom of
the wok to release any spices which may be stuck.*

Kari Daging
(Beef Curry)

2 medium-sized
  potatoes
500 ml (2 cups) water
5 shallots, or 1 onion
5 cloves garlic
2 cm (3/4 in) fresh
  ginger
3 tablespoons meat
  curry powder
4 tablespoons oil
5 cm (2 in) cinnamon
4 cardamom pods,
  bruised
2 whole star anise
6 cloves
1 sprig curry leaves
400–500 g (1 lb) lean
  topside beef, in 1-cm
  (1/2-in) slices, about
  3 cm (1 1/4 in) square
2 large ripe tomatoes,
  cut in wedges
250 ml (1 cup) coconut
  milk
Salt to taste

1. Peel potatoes and cut into 2-cm (3/4-in) chunks. Place in a small pan, cover with water and cook until just tender, 8 to 10 minutes. Drain, saving cooking water. Combine curry powder with 85 ml (1/3 cup) of the reserved water in a small bowl. Keep remaining water.

2. While potatoes are cooking, process shallots, garlic and ginger to a smooth paste in a spice grinder, adding a little of the oil if required to keep the mixture turning.

3. Heat oil in a medium pan. Add cinnamon, cardamom, star anise, cloves and curry leaves and stir-fry for over low heat, 1 minute. Add the processed mixture and cook over low heat, 3 minutes. Add curry paste and cook, stirring frequently until dry, about 3 to 4 minutes.

4. Add the beef sauté over low heat, 10 minutes. Add tomatoes into wedges and sauté 10 minutes, scraping up any spice paste stuck to the bottom of the pan as tomatoes soften.

5. Add 250 ml (1 cup) of the reserved potato water. Bring to the boil, cover, then simmer until beef is tender, about 45 minutes, adding more water if required. Add potatoes and coconut milk and simmer uncovered for 10 minutes. Season to taste with salt and serve.

Serves 4
Preparation time: 20 mins
Cooking time: 1 hour 30 mins

Kerutuk
(Dry Spicy Beef Curry)

600 g (1 1/4 lb) beef topside, in 2 cm (3/4 in) slices
1 tablespoon dried tamarind pulp
125 ml (1/2 cup) warm water
3 tablespoons oil
4 cardamom pods, bruised
6 cloves
3 cm (1 1/4 in) cinnamon
1 whole star anise
1 cm (1/2 in) fresh ginger, shredded
3 cloves garlic, sliced
4 shallots, sliced
300 ml (1 1/4 cups) thick coconut milk
2 teaspoons sugar
Salt to taste

Spice Paste
100 g (1 cup loosely-packed) grated coconut
2 tablespoons oil
2 1/2 tablespoons coriander
1 1/4 tablespoons cumin
1 1/4 tablespoons fennel
15–20 dried chillies, cut in 3-cm (1 1/4-in) pieces
3 cm (1 1/4 in) galangal, coarsely chopped
6 shallots, coarsely chopped
5 cloves garlic, coarsely chopped

1. To prepare spice paste, dry-fry the grated coconut in a wok over low heat until crisp and golden brown, 6 to 8 minutes. Grind to the texture of fine breadcrumbs, then transfer to a bowl

2. Put coriander, cumin and fennel in the dry wok and stir-fry over low heat, 1 minute. Grind to a powder in a spice grinder, then add to coconut. Heat oil in wok, add the galangal, chillies, shallots and garlic and fry until golden brown, 2 to 3 minutes. Grind to a smooth paste in a spice grinder or blender, then add to coconut and spices; mix well.

3. Cut beef in 4 x 6 cm (1 1/2 x 2 1/2 in) pieces. Mix thoroughly with spice paste and marinate 30 minutes. While beef is marinating, mix tamarind and warm water. Soak 5 minutes, then squeeze and strain to obtain tamarind juice. Set aside.

4. Heat oil in the wok and fry the cardamoms, cloves, cinnamon and star anise over low heat, 2 to 3 minutes. Add ginger, garlic and shallots and fry until golden brown, 2 to 3 minutes. Add beef and stir-fry 2 to 3 minutes, taking care not to burn coconut.

5. Add the coconut milk and tamarind juice and bring to the boil, stirring. Cover wok, reduce heat and simmer until beef is tender and gravy is quite thick, 1 to 1 1/4 hours. Adding a little water if mixture threatens to stick and burn before meat is cooked. Season to taste with sugar and salt and serve with rice.

If preferred, shake out some or all of the seeds from the dried chillies to reduce the heat.

Serves 4
Preparation time: **1 hour**
Cooking time: **1 hour 30 mins**

Daging Goreng Bercili
(Chilli-fried Beef)

500 g (1 1/4 lb) rump or topside beef

6–12 dried chillies, cut in 2 cm (3/4 in) pieces

3–6 fresh red chillies, sliced

6 shallots, chopped

2 cloves garlic, chopped

125 ml (1/2 cup) oil

2 cm (3/4 in) fresh ginger, shredded

2 medium-sized onions, thinly sliced across

1 tablespoon lime juice

2 teaspoons sugar

1 teaspoon salt

1. Cut the beef into pieces, approximately 6 x 4 x 4 cm (2 1/2 x 1 1/2 x 1 1/2 in). Put in a pan, add water to cover and bring to the boil. Skim off any scum that rises, lower heat, cover and simmer until beef is very tender, about 1 1/4 to 1 1/2 hours. Drain beef, reserving stock for some other use. When beef is cool, cut in 1/2-cm (1/4-in) slices.

2. Soak chillies in warm water until soft, 10 to 15 minutes. Process soaked chillies, red chillies, shallots and garlic to a smooth paste in a spice grinder or electric blender, adding a little oil if needed to keep the mixture turning.

3. Set aside 4 tablespoons of the oil. Heat remainder in a wok and stir-fry half the beef over very high heat until lightly browned all over, about 2 minutes. Remove and drain on paper towel. Repeat with remaining beef.

4. Reduce heat to moderate and stir-fry the onion rings until translucent, about 2 minutes. Drain on paper towel. Add ginger to wok and stir-fry until golden brown, about 1 minute.

5. Add reserved 4 tablespoons oil to the wok and add chilli paste. Stir over low heat until the mixture is fragrant and oil separates, 5 to 6 minutes. Add salt, sugar and lime juice.

6. Return the beef, onion and ginger to the wok and add salt, sugar and lime juice. Stir-fry over moderate heat until beef is well coated with the chilli paste, 1 to 2 minutes. Serve.

To reduce the heat of this dish, use fewer chillies and remove some or all of the seeds.

Serves 4
Preparation time: **20 mins**
Cooking time: **1 1/2 to 2 hours**

Rendang Daging
(Beef Rendang)

- 100 g (1 cup loosely packed) freshly grated or desiccated coconut
- 12–15 dried chillies, cut in 2-cm (3/4-in) pieces
- 15 shallots, chopped
- 2 cm (3/4 in) fresh ginger, chopped
- 2 cm (3/4 in) galangal, chopped
- 3 stems lemongrass, bottom 10 cm (4 in) only, thinly sliced
- 1 cm (1/2 in) fresh turmeric root, chopped, or 1/2 teaspoon ground turmeric
- 625 ml (2 1/2 cups) coconut milk
- 250 ml (1 cup) water
- 1 tablespoon dried tamarind pulp
- 500 g (1 lb) lean topside or other stewing beef, cut in bite-sized pieces
- 4 tablespoons warm water
- 1 small turmeric leaf, coarsely torn, optional
- 2 kaffir lime leaves, edges torn
- 2 teaspoons sugar
- 1–2 teaspoons salt

1. Put grated coconut in a wok and cook over low heat, tossing and stirring until coconut is crisp and golden brown, about 20 minutes. Cool slightly before processing to the texture of fine breadcrumbs. Set aside.
2. Soak dried chillies in warm water until soft, 10 to 15 minutes. Drain, discarding as many of the seeds as possible. Process chillies, shallots, ginger, galangal, lemongrass and turmeric root to a smooth paste in a spice grinder or blender, adding little of the coconut milk as needed to keep the mixture turning.
3. Put processed mixture in a wok or wide pan, and add beef, remaining coconut milk and 250 ml (1 cup) water. Bring mixture to a boil, stirring constantly. Reduce heat and simmer, stirring occasionally until the beef is tender, about 1 to 1 1/4 hours, adding a little more water if the sauce threatens to dry out before the beef is cooked. At the end of cooking, most of the liquid will have evaporated and a red film of oil risen to the surface
4. Soak tamarind pulp in water for 5 minutes, then squeeze and strain to obtain the juice. Add the juice, turmeric leaf, kaffir lime leaves, sugar and salt to the pan. Cook for 5 minutes, stirring frequently, then serve.

Lamb could be used instead of beef if preferred. If using a spice grinder to process the spice paste, you may need to process half the ingredients at a time.

Serves 4
Preparation time: **40 mins**
Cooking time: **1 hour**

Masak Lemak Daging
(Beef & Potatoes in Coconut Gravy)

3 fresh red chillies, chopped

6–8 bird's-eye chillies, chopped

2 cloves garlic, chopped

1 cm (1/2 in) fresh ginger, chopped

1 cm (1/2 in) fresh turmeric root, chopped, or 1/4 teaspoon ground turmeric

500 g (1 lb) rump steak, thinly sliced

400 ml (1 2/3 cups) coconut milk (extracted from 1/2 coconut)

3 cm (1 1/4 in) galangal, bruised

1 stalk lemongrass, bottom 10 cm (4 in) only, bruised

2 kaffir lime leaves, roughly torn

2 medium-sized potatoes, cut in 2 cm (3/4 in) cubes

2 dried tamarind slices (*asam keping/asam gelugor*), or 1 table-spoon dried tamarind pulp

1 teaspoon salt

1. Process the chillies, garlic, ginger and turmeric to a smooth paste in a spice grinder, adding a little water if necessary to keep the mixture turning.
2. Put the chilli paste and beef in a pan and cook over medium heat, stirring occasionally, until the beef sweats and the liquid dries up completely, 8 to 10 minutes.
3. Add the coconut milk, galangal, lemongrass and kaffir lime leaves. Bring to the boil, stirring constantly, then lower heat and simmer uncovered for 10 minutes.
4. Add potatoes and simmer over low heat until potatoes are just tender, about 15 minutes. Add the tamarind slices and salt and simmer 10 minutes.

If using dried tamarind pulp, soak in 4 tablespoons of warm water 5 minutes, then squeeze and strain to obtain tamarind juice. Add in step 4.

Serves 4
Preparation time: **15 mins**
Cooking time: **35 mins**

Serunding Daging
(Spicy Dried Shredded Beef)

500 g (1 lb) shin or top-
  side beef
10–12 dried chillies, cut
  in 2-cm (3/4-in) pieces
10 shallots, chopped
4 1/2 cm (3/4 in) fresh
  ginger, chopped
3 stems lemongrass,
  inner part of bottom
  10 cm (4 in) only, thinly
  sliced
1 cm (1/2 in) fresh
  turmeric root, chopped,
  or 1/2 teaspoon
  ground turmeric
1 cm (1/2 in) galangal,
  chopped
300 ml (1 1/4 cups)
  thick coconut milk
1 1/2 teaspoons salt
1 dried tamarind slice
  (*asam keping/asam
  gelugor*), or 2 tea-
  spoons dried tamarind
  pulp, soaked in 2 tablespoons water,
  squeezed and strained
  to obtain juice

1. Cut beef into 6-cm (2 1/2-in) cubes. Put in a pan, add water to just cover and bring to the boil. Cover, lower heat and simmer until just tender, 45 to 60 minutes. Drain, reserving stock. When beef is cool enough to handle, use the fingers to tear the meat along the grain to make fine, hair-like shreds.

2. Soak chillies in warm water to soften, 10 to 15 minutes; discard some of the seeds to reduce heat if liked. Process chillies, shallots, ginger, lemongrass, turmeric and galangal to a coarse paste in a spice grinder or blender. Gradually add 180 ml (3/4 cup) of the reserved beef stock and keep blending until smooth.

3. Stir-fry processed mixture, coconut milk and salt in a large wok over medium heat until the mixture is very thick and starting to dry out, about 15 minutes.

4. Add the shredded beef. Reduce heat to very low heat and cook beef, stirring and tossing frequently, 30 minutes.

5. Add the tamarind slices or tamarind juice and continue cooking until the meat is completely dry and crisp, 20 to 30 minutes. Allow to cool thoroughly before storing in an airtight container. Serve as a garnish with rice and other dishes.

The beef will keep for several weeks at room temperature, provided a clean, dry spoon is used each time some of the beef is removed.

Serves 4
Preparation time: **1 hour**
Cooking time: **2 hours**

Lepat Pisang
(Steamed Banana Cakes)

18–20 pieces banana leaf, or aluminium foil, 12 x 10 cm (5 x 4 in)
4 very ripe bananas, about 400 g (13 oz)
70 g (1/2 cup + 1 tablespoon) plain flour
30 g (1/4 cup) cornflour
70 g (1/3 cup + 1 tablespoon) finely chopped palm sugar
4 tablespoons thick coconut milk
Pinch of salt

1. Soften banana leaves by dipping into boiling water 30 seconds. Drain and wipe dry with paper towel.
2. Mash the bananas. Stir in the flour, cornflour, sugar, coconut milk and salt, adding more coconut milk if required to give a soft, dropping consistency. If too moist, add a little more plain flour.
3. Work with one banana leaf piece at a time. Position it, long side facing you. Place one heaped tablespoon of banana mixture in the centre and fold, overlapping both sides, to enclose the mixture. Tuck both ends under. Continue wrapping until banana mixture is used up.
4. Lay the packets in a single layer in a steamer. Put over rapidly boiling water and steam 20 minutes, adding more boiling water after 10 minutes. Serve warm, or at room temperature.

Take care when cutting the banana leaf as the sap from the central rib will stain.

Serves 4
Preparation time: **30 mins**
Cooking time: **20 mins**

With the long side facing you, place 1 heaped tablespoon banana mixture in the centre.

Fold the leaf, overlapping both sides, then fold the ends underneath.

Bubur Kacang
(Mung Bean Dessert)

200 g (1 cup) dried mung beans (*kacang hijau*)
1 1/2 litres water
2 pandanus leaves, or 2 drops pandan essence
1 1/2 tablespoons pearl sago (optional)
4 tablespoons coconut cream
1/4 teaspoon salt
125 g (3/4 cup) roughly chopped palm sugar
1–3 tablespoons white sugar

Serves 4
Preparation time: **40 mins**
Cooking time: **1 hour**

1. Pick the beans over for grit and foreign particles. Rinse in several changes of water. Place beans in a large pan and add water. Leave to soak 30 minutes.
2. Rake leaves with a fork and tie each into a knot. Add to pan. Bring to the boil, reduce heat, cover and simmer until beans are tender, about 45 minutes.
3. If using sago, place in a small sieve and rinse under running water. When beans are quite tender, add sago. Simmer uncovered, stirring occasionally, until the sago is clear and swollen, about 15 minutes.
4. Remove pandanus leaves, then add the coconut cream, salt, palm sugar and white sugar to taste. Cook gently, stirring, until sugar has dissolved, 1 to 2 minutes. Serve warm or cold.

Cook beans in pressure cooker for 20 mins (use only 750 ml water). If not using sago, simmer beans uncovered 15 mins in step 3 to thicken dessert.

Pengat Labu
(Pumpkin in Sweetened Coconut Milk)

600 g (1 1/4 lb) orange-skinned pumpkin

2 pandanus leaves, or few drops pandan essence

150 g (1 cup) coarsely chopped palm sugar

500 ml (2 cups) thick coconut milk

Generous pinch of salt

Serves 4

Preparation time: **10 mins**

Cooking time: **20 mins**

1. Peel the pumpkin and cut into 2-cm (3/4-in) chunks. Set aside.

2. Rake pandanus leaves with a fork, then tie each into a knot.

3. Put palm sugar, coconut milk, pandanus leaves and salt into a medium-sized saucepan. Heat gently, uncovered, stirring constantly to stop the coconut milk curdling.

4. When the palm sugar has dissolved, add the pumpkin and cook uncovered over low heat, stirring several times, until pumpkin is tender but not mushy, about 15 minutes. Serve warm or at room temperature.

Index